Sandy Creek
NEW YORK

An Imprint of Sterling Publishing
1166 Avenue of The Americas
New York, NY, 10036

First published in 2013 by Hodder Children's Books,
an imprint of Hachette Children's Group

Illustrations © 2013 by Zdenko Basic and Manuel Šumberac
This 2014 edition published by Sandy Creek.

ISBN 978-1-4351-6188-7
Manufactured in China
Lot #:
2 4 6 8 10 9 7 5 3 1
08/15

The Night Before Christmas

Written by Clement C. Moore

Illustrated by Zdenko Basic and Manuel Šumberac

Sandy Creek
NEW YORK

'TWAS THE NIGHT BEFORE CHRISTMAS,
WHEN ALL THROUGH THE HOUSE
Not a creature was stirring, not even a mouse.
The stockings were hung by the chimney with care,
In hopes that Saint Nicholas soon would be there.

The children were nestled all snug in their beds,
While visions of sugarplums danced in their heads.
And Mama in her 'kerchief and I in my cap
Had just settled down for a long winter's nap.

When out on the lawn there arose such a clatter,
I sprang from my bed to see what was the matter.
Away to the window I flew like a flash,
Tore open the shutters and threw up the sash.

The moon on the breast of the new-fallen snow
Gave the luster of midday to objects below,
When what to my wondering eyes should appear,
But a miniature sleigh and eight tiny reindeer,
With a little old driver so lively and quick,
I knew in a moment it must be Saint Nick!

More rapid than eagles his coursers they came,
And he whistled and shouted and called them by name:
"Now, Dasher! Now, Dancer! Now, Prancer and Vixen!
On, Comet! On, Cupid! On, Donner and Blitzen!
To the top of the porch, to the top of the wall!
Now dash away! Dash away! Dash away, all!"

As dry leaves that before the wild hurricane fly,
When they meet with an obstacle, mount to the sky,
So up to the housetop the coursers they flew,
With sleigh full of toys and Saint Nicholas, too.
And then, in a twinkling, I heard on the roof
The prancing and pawing of each little hoof.

He was dressed
all in fur from
his head to his foot,
And his clothes were
all tarnished with
ashes and soot.

As I drew in
my head and
was turning around,
Down the chimney
Saint Nicholas
came with a bound.

A bundle of toys he had flung on his back,
And he looked like a peddler just opening his pack.
His eyes how they twinkled! His dimples how merry!
His cheeks were like roses, his nose like a cherry!

His droll little mouth was drawn up like a bow,
And the beard on his chin was as white as the snow.
The stump of a pipe he held tight in his teeth,
And the smoke, it encircled his head like a wreath.

He had a broad face and a little round belly
That shook when he laughed like a bowl full of jelly.
He was chubby and plump, a right jolly old elf,

And I laughed when I saw him, in spite of myself.
A wink of his eye and a twist of his head
Soon gave me to know I had nothing to dread.

He spoke not a word, but went straight to his work,
And filled all the stockings, then turned with a jerk,

And laying his finger aside of his nose,
And giving a nod, up the chimney he rose.

He sprang to his sleigh, to his team gave a whistle,
And away they all flew like the down of a thistle.

But I heard him exclaim ere he drove out of sight,
"MERRY CHRISTMAS TO ALL,
AND TO ALL A GOOD NIGHT!"